# POMPEII
## LOST & FOUND

By **MARY POPE OSBORNE**
Frescoes by **BONNIE CHRISTENSEN**

Alfred A. Knopf
NEW YORK

ALMOST 2,000 YEARS AGO, POMPEII was a thriving Roman town on the Mediterranean Sea. The town was just six miles below a huge volcano named Mount Vesuvius. But the people of Pompeii paid little attention to the looming mountain. They were busy tending to their homes and families, going to work or school, enjoying theater or gladiator contests, and gossiping with their friends at the public baths.

As everyone went about their daily routines on August 24, AD 79, no one seemed to notice that strange things had begun to happen. The sea had become choppy. In nearby fields, streams had dried up. Cattle were moaning and birds had stopped singing. Inside the town walls, dogs were howling. And from the top of Mount Vesuvius, smoke was streaming.

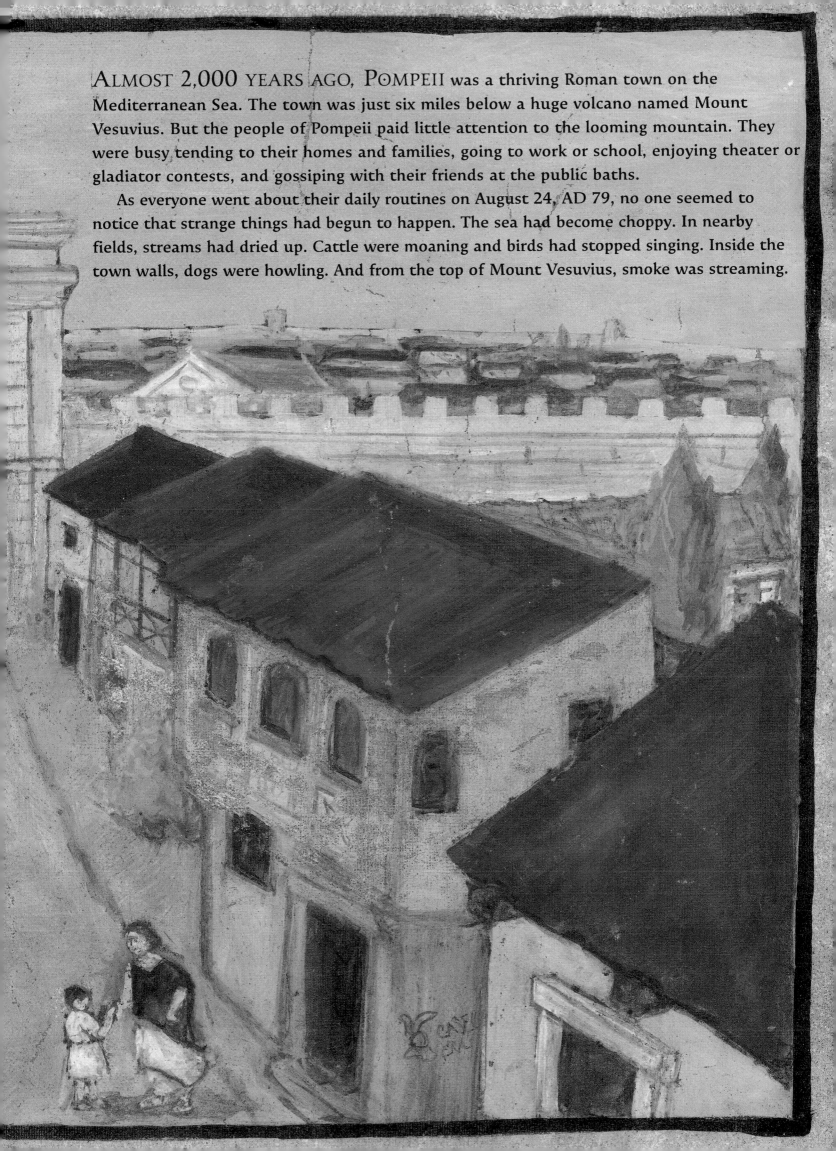

In the early afternoon, a huge blast shattered the
air. People rushed out of shops and houses to see
what was happening. A great plume of smoke and
fire was billowing up from Vesuvius. Volcanic stones
began bombarding the town. The sky was so thick
with ash that darkness fell, turning day to night.
People shouted and screamed; they thought it was
the end of the world. They raised their hands to the
heavens and prayed to the Roman gods.

Over the next eighteen hours, poisonous gases
filled the air. Tons of hot ash rained down on
Pompeii until the town was completely buried.

For over 1,500 years, the world forgot the town that had been buried by the hot ash from Mount Vesuvius. Shepherds never suspected that beneath the grassy fields where their sheep grazed lay the ruins of a prosperous Roman town.

One day in the late 1500s, diggers working on an underground canal uncovered the ruins of wall paintings and slabs of marble. The architect who led the project believed the ruins were part of an ancient Italian villa. Later, in the 1600s, many more ruins were unearthed. But it was not until 1763 that an inscription positively identified the lost town of Pompeii.

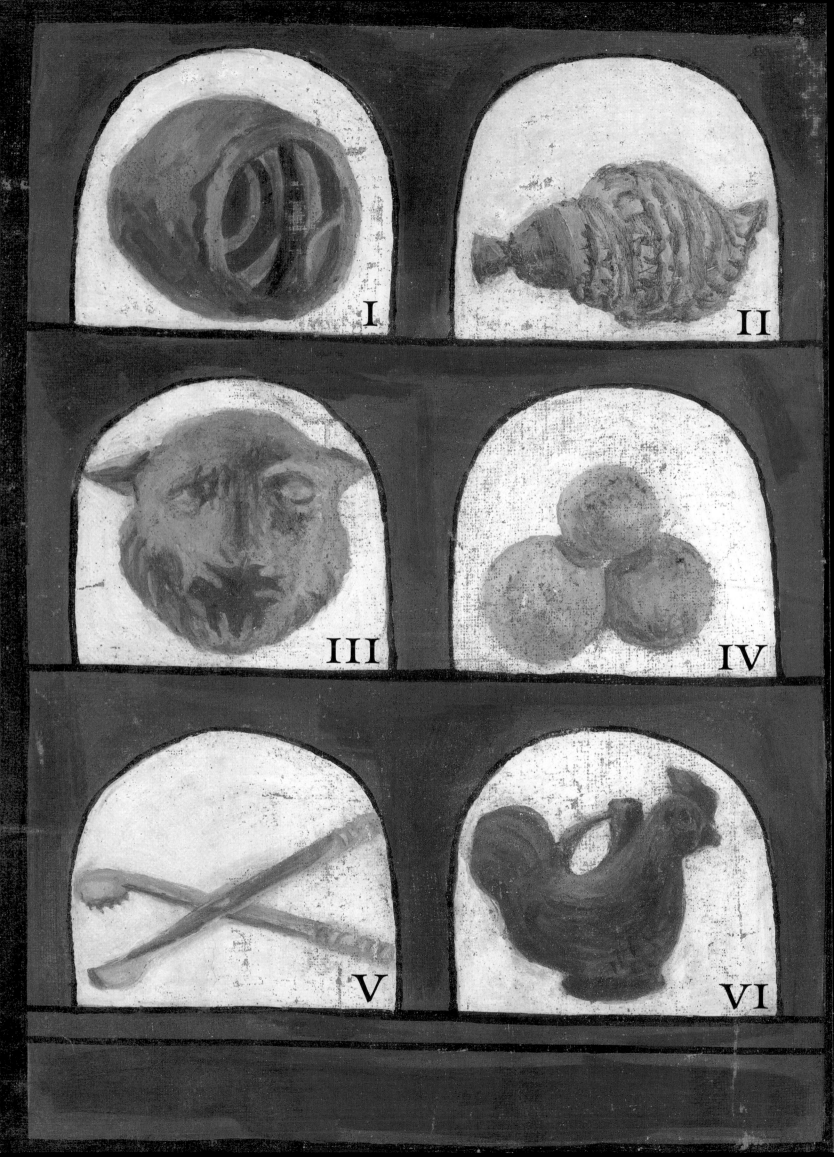

Since then, archaeologists have uncovered about two-thirds of Pompeii. They've found the ruins of many buildings, as well as thousands of everyday objects. They've even discovered food and the seeds of garden flowers preserved in the ashes. Archaeologists have found graffiti scrawled on walls throughout the town. And they've uncovered countless wall paintings, called frescoes, which show scenes from daily life. The graffiti helps us hear the "voices" of the lost people of Pompeii, and the frescoes help us imagine what they looked like and how they dressed.

❖

*Pictured on the facing page are objects that were found in the ruins. Can you guess how they were used? The answers are at the end of the book.*

Archaeologists have found an even more accurate way to show us what the people of Pompeii looked like. After the volcano erupted, thousands were buried under the ash that fell from the sky. Eventually their bodies decayed, leaving empty spaces inside the hardened ash. By pouring plaster into these spaces, archaeologists have made statues of some of the people and animals of Pompeii.

The plaster shapes reveal family members huddled together, their faces twisted with pain and fear. They show people holding lamps, trying to find their way through the terrible darkness. One shape reveals a watchdog, struggling to break free from his chain.

With all the discoveries of the archaeologists, we can now fully imagine what everyday life was like in a Roman town almost 2,000 years ago.

We know that all kinds of people lived in Pompeii: wealthy Romans who vacationed in grand villas with beautiful gardens, craftspeople who lived in homes behind their workshops, and slaves who worked endless hours and slept in small, bare rooms.

◆

*Found: Garden tools, looking very much like our rakes and spades of today.*

Of course, there was no modern heating or electricity in any of the houses of Pompeii. People warmed their homes with smoky coal-burning heaters. At night, light from their candles and oil lamps lit the dark.

Many houses had small, high windows designed to keep out burglars. Often there was a large opening in the ceiling to let in sunlight. Rainwater fell through it into a basin below. This water was used by the household for cooking and washing.

At dinner, wealthy families reclined on couches while slaves served them food. The people of Pompeii enjoyed eating fish and lamb, fruit, and bread. Archaeologists have uncovered many bakeries in Pompeii with petrified loaves of bread still in their ovens!

*Found: A loaf of bread and a glass pitcher.*

In early Roman times, slavery was a fact of life. Of the 20,000 people who lived in Pompeii, perhaps as many as 8,000 were slaves. The most famous people of Pompeii were a special group of slaves and prisoners—the gladiators. Archaeologists have uncovered gladiators' helmets (like the one shown below), swords, and armor. They've also found graffiti written about gladiators, such as "Celadus, glory of the girls, heartthrob of the girls."

Though gladiators were as celebrated as movie stars today, they lived desperate lives. In the town's huge amphitheater, they fought bloody battles with each other. A wounded fighter lived or died according to the will of the crowd. If the audience wanted him to live, they gave a "thumbs up" sign. If they wanted him to die, they gave a "thumbs down" sign.

The people of Pompeii loved going to concerts and plays that were performed in outdoor theaters. Many musical instruments have been found among the ruins, including pipes, rattles, and cymbals. Wall paintings show actors wearing masks while they perform. Funny characters wore masks with big smiles, while tragic characters wore mournful frowns.

The public baths of Pompeii were also places of great activity. Many men and women enjoyed frequent visits to the baths. There, they washed themselves and used toilets that actually had running water. They exercised, lifted weights, played ball, and swam in pools. They even bowled in bowling alleys! The baths were a good place to meet with friends, gossip, and discuss politics.

*Found: An ancient "bath kit" consisting of a flask for oil, scrapers, and a spoon for oil or water.*

While grown-ups played in the public baths, the children of Pompeii played in the narrow cobblestone streets or in sunny courtyards. They sailed wooden boats and played with dolls, balls, and marbles.

Many children went to school to learn Latin, Greek, arithmetic, and public speaking. They wrote on wax-coated tablets with sharp tools. Instead of reading books, they read from scrolls of paper made from reeds.

*Found: Bronze sculpture of a dove.*
*Doves were popular pets for children.*

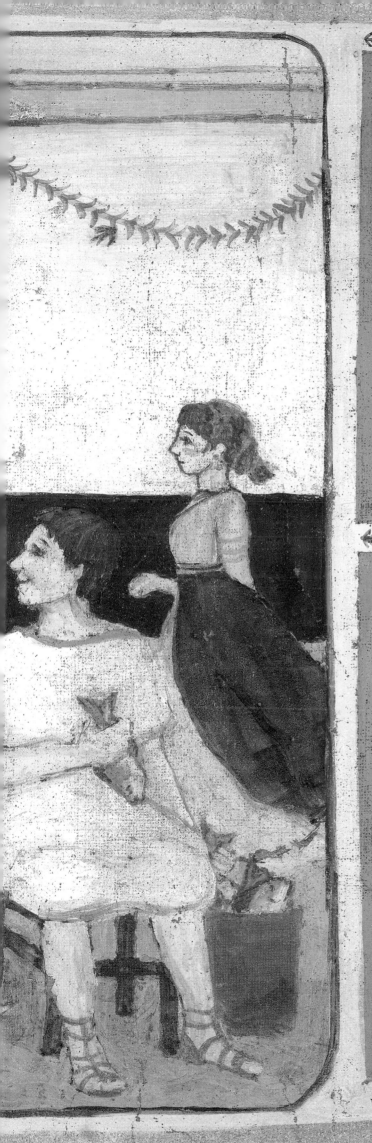

The main shopping in Pompeii was done at a big, bustling outdoor market called the forum. The forum had stalls where shoppers could buy almost anything, from shoes and figs to sheep and pigeons. The most delectable items were fish fresh from the sea, wine from the vineyards on the hills beneath Vesuvius, and olive oil from Pompeii's renowned olive groves.

The forum was not only a lively place for shopping. There were also courts of law there and temples where people worshiped the Roman gods and goddesses.

*Found: Scales and gold coins.*

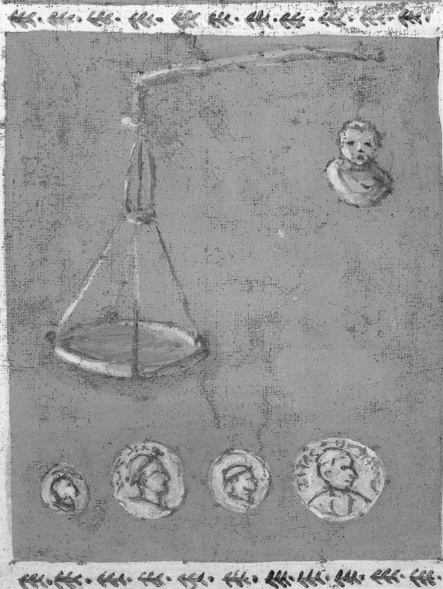

The people of Pompeii had many gods and goddesses. They worshiped them in temples and kept small shrines in their houses. Their most important gods were Jupiter, the king of the gods, and Apollo, the god of light. Venus, the goddess of love, was considered the special protector of Pompeii. She was painted on many walls throughout the town. She appeared on election posters and was woven into cloth. One cloth maker portrayed Venus and her son Cupid in a chariot pulled by elephants.

◈

*Found: Stone statue of Jupiter.*

On August 24, AD 79, people were strolling through the narrow cobblestone streets of Pompeii on their way to the temples, the forum, and the public baths.

Suddenly, in the early afternoon, a terrible explosion shattered the air . . .

. . . and the town of Pompeii became frozen in time forever.

Archaeologists continue to uncover more and more of lost Pompeii. Of the 20,000 people who lived there, the remains of about 2,000 have been unearthed. Many people fled the town on foot. But it is now believed that those who escaped most likely died in the dark countryside when tons of hot ash fell from the sky. No one will ever know how many people of Pompeii perished during those terrible hours in AD 79.

# ✳ THE MAKING OF FRESCOES ✳

Fresco is a painting technique that has been used for thousands of years. Today frescoes still decorate the walls in the ruins of ancient Pompeii.

The first step in making a fresco is to apply a layer of wet plaster to a wall or panel. After transferring a drawing onto the painting area, the artist paints with pure pigment (color) mixed with water. The painting must be completed while the plaster is wet, or fresh. The word "fresh" is *fresco* in Italian.

As the plaster dries, a chemical reaction permanently bonds the pigment painting to the wall or panel.

When dried, the fresco can be pulled from the wall or panel and mounted on linen. The complicated process is called *strappo d'affresco* and gives the fresco an aged look.

—Bonnie Christensen
January 2006

# ✳ ANSWERS TO FOUND ITEMS ✳

**I**     *Dormouse house. Dormice were considered a delicacy by the people of Pompeii, who raised them for food.*

**II**     *Bugle. Pompeiians made bugles from the shells of large gastropods that lived in the Mediterranean Sea.*

**III**     *Bear water spout. Water spouts were attached to lead pipes that drained water. In this case, water would spurt out of the bear's mouth.*

**IV**     *Catapult balls. These catapult balls made from volcanic stone were probably used in the siege of Pompeii by Rome in 89 BC.*

**V**     *Tooth extractor. The doctors of Pompeii used sophisticated tools for medicine and dentistry.*

**VI**     *Chicken pitcher. This pitcher in the shape of a chicken is made of clay and is much like pitchers made in Italy today.*

*To Will and Caroline Boyce*
*—M.P.O.*

*For Janet Schulman*
*—B.C.*

# ❋ ACKNOWLEDGMENTS ❋

Many, many thanks to Matilde Dolcetti and the Scuola Internazionale di Grafica in Venice, Italy, for their kind and generous support and to fresco artist Silvestro Lodi.
Also thanks to Saint Michael's College in Colchester, Vermont, and to Lance Richbourg.
And to Viola Dominello for carrying forty pounds of linen the length of Italy.
—Bonnie Christensen

THIS IS A BORZOI BOOK PUBLISHED BY ALFRED A. KNOPF

Text copyright © 2006 by Mary Pope Osborne
Illustrations copyright © 2006 by Bonnie Christensen

All rights reserved under International and Pan-American Copyright Conventions. Published in the United States by Alfred A. Knopf, an imprint of Random House Children's Books, a division of Random House, Inc., New York, and simultaneously in Canada by Random House of Canada Limited, Toronto. Distributed by Random House, Inc., New York. KNOPF, BORZOI BOOKS, and the colophon are registered trademarks of Random House, Inc.
www.randomhouse.com/kids

Library of Congress Cataloging-in-Publication Data
Osborne, Mary Pope.
Pompeii : lost and found / by Mary Pope Osborne ; frescoes by Bonnie Christensen.
p. cm.
"This is a Borzoi book."
ISBN 0-375-82889-3 (trade) — ISBN 0-375-92889-8 (lib. bdg.)
1. Pompeii (Extinct city)—Juvenile literature. I. Christensen, Bonnie. II. Title.
DG70.P708 2006
937'.7—dc22
2005009331

MANUFACTURED IN CHINA
January 2006
10 9 8 7 6 5 4 3 2 1
First Edition